Forging my Own Path

Triumphs and Trials of Resilience

LaFortune Djabea

Title: Forging my Own Path: Triumphs and Trials of Resilience

Subtitle

-

Contributors LaFortune Djabea
ISBN 9798868957871 (sc)
ISBN 9798868957888 (e)

Imprint: Ingram Sparks

Edition

Edition Statement (5 / 255) First

Cover design By LaNoya Corley
Front Cover photograph by Leah Jayne Production
Edited and Formatted by Polgarus Studio

For Leandra and Shelton and Alenna...
And, of course, my mother and my Grandmother

Contents

“Delight yourself also in the Lord, and he shall give you the desires of your heart”

_Psalm 103:5

Preface:

The absence of my father and the constant shuffling between different homes left me feeling like a perpetual outsider. The early years without my mother's presence had a profound impact on my self-worth and confidence, causing me to question why my parents chose to abandon me.

I learned to rely on myself and developed a strong sense of independence. The constant feeling of being an outcast pushed me to prove my worth to the world. I poured my energy into my studies, excelling academically to compensate for the emotional void in my life.

As I grew older, I realized that my worth was not defined by the actions of others. I began to understand that my parents' choices did not determine my value as a person. It was a difficult realization, but it allowed me to let go of the burden of their abandonment.

Instead of dwelling on the past, I focused on building a future of which I could be proud.

I found solace in knowing that my experiences could make a positive impact on someone else's life.

With each passing day, I grew more resilient. I learned to embrace being unique and celebrate the strength that came from overcoming adversity. The scars of my past became a testament to that resilience, reminding me of the battles I had fought and conquered.

Today, I stand tall and confident in my own skin. The journey of self-discovery has taught me that I have not been defined by the circumstances of my upbringing—I am defined by the person I have become, the values I hold, and the love and compassion I share with others.

The absence of my parents will always be a part of my story, but I have found my own path, one filled with love, purpose, and a will to make a difference. And as I continue to grow and evolve, I am grateful for the strength I gained from my past, for it has shaped me into the resilient individual I am today.

Gratitude fills my heart for the life I have lived thus far, recognizing that as long as I am breathing, there is an abundance of untapped experiences awaiting me. Our journey is not solely mapped by the trials we have faced, but rather by the endless possibilities that lie ahead, beckoning us with open arms. My journey is far from over.

No longer will I be held back by fear or doubt. Instead, I will approach each new experience with a sense of wonder and curiosity. I will welcome the unknown, knowing that it is through these future experiences that I will truly discover who I am and of what I am capable.

Life is a tapestry of moments, both big and small, and I must make each one count. I will savor the simple joys, the laughter shared with loved ones, and the beauty found in the world around me.

Family dynamics:

Throughout my childhood, I was forever caught in a whirlwind of unpredictability and instability. Moving from one place to another became the norm, leaving me with a profound sense of displacement and a constant desire for stability that felt unattainable. However, amidst the chaos of my upbringing, there was one enigma that haunted me for years—the identity of my biological father.

In our household, the mere mention of my father was strictly forbidden. It was as if his existence had been erased, and no one dared to utter his name. This veil of secrecy slowly corroded my spirit, as I yearned to unravel the mystery of who he was and why he was absent from my life. Having no paternal figure created a void within me, a void that I desperately sought to fill with love and acceptance from others. As I grew older, I realized that family isn't just blood relations. It is the people who stand by you, who love and support you unconditionally, that truly matter.

Although the mystery of my father's identity still lingered in the back of my mind, I focused on building a life filled with love, purpose, and stability. I pursued my passions, worked hard to create a stable career, and nurtured the relationships that brought me joy and fulfillment.

In time, I came to understand that these circumstances shaped me into a resilient and independent individual. It taught me the importance of self-reliance and the power of forging my own path. I no longer yearned for a father's presence, for I had found strength within myself and the support of my chosen family.

The enigma of my father's identity may always remain unsolved. I have come to peace with that. Instead, I now challenge uncertainty and focus on the love and stability that I have created in my life.

Life was unpredictable and unstable in my childhood. Still, I have emerged from it with a deep appreciation for the stability and love, and a sense of belonging that I once thought unattainable.

Growing up as the black sheep of my family, I always felt like an outsider. My unique interests, introverted personality, and inability to fit into their predetermined mold cemented my outcast status. This perception of being on the outskirts of my own family only intensified my yearning for connection and acceptance.

To complicate matters further, my mother was also absent for a significant portion of my early years. At the tender age of three, she made the decision to venture overseas, leaving me in the care of others. This choice had profound consequences, as I was shuffled from one temporary home to another, never truly finding a place to call my own. It took a toll on my emotional well-being, leaving me susceptible to the physical and emotional abuse I endured as a child.

It was the catalyst for a series of poor relationship choices later in my life. I sought love and validation in all the wrong places, hoping to fill that *void.* It took an abusive marriage and several failed relationships for me to realize the impact that my parents' absence had on my self-esteem and my ability to form healthy connections.

Seeking help through counseling became a turning point. It was through therapy that I began to rebuild myself and reclaim my power. I learned that I was worthy of love and respect, regardless of my family background. I could be whole and complete on my own, without relying on a man—any man—to measure my worth.

The rejection and hurtful words hurled at me by family members only fueled my will to rise above the pain. I refused to hear their words. Instead, I used their negativity to trigger resilience, propelling me forward on a path of self-discovery and personal growth.

In sharing my memoir, I hope to inspire others who have experienced similar hardships. I want to show them that they too can overcome the wounds of their past and find their own path to healing and self-discovery. Together, we can embrace our stories, find our voices, and rewrite our narratives with strength, resilience, and unwavering self-worth.

Coming to the USA—the move:

As the clock struck 10:00 PM, my newly acquired petite suitcase stood prepared, marking the beginning of an enigmatic expedition. I had purchased it just the day before, eager to embark on a journey that would take me from Cameroon to Paris, with a subsequent voyage to the United States the following day. The secrecy surrounding my departure was paramount; I was strictly instructed not to disclose the details to anyone in my hometown. However, my notorious inability to keep quiet led me to spill the beans to my closest friends, revealing my pursuit of a better life in America. My mother, aware of my tendency to divulge secrets, often pondered how I managed to safeguard others' confidences while failing to protect my own.

A few years later there would be a particular secret I concealed from her after moving to Massachusetts from Georgia for ten months. Eventually, the truth had to be unveiled, as the impending arrival of my daughter necessitated my confession—just a month before my mother would undoubtedly discover it for herself.

When I arrived in the United States, I was young and

unfamiliar with anyone in the country except for a friend introduced to me by a mutual acquaintance just a few days before. With less than $300 to my name, I needed a place to stay for a while. When my plane landed in Washington DC, I had to catch my first Greyhound bus to Atlanta, Georgia. Exhausted and with limited knowledge of English, I couldn't sleep out of fear that something might happen to me. Clutching my small suitcase, I counted the few dollars I had in my hand, hoping to buy some food. Armed with my tickets, I approached the teller to inquire about my bus and explain where I was headed. It was a challenge to understand the intercom announcements, and I strained to catch a few words. I remember going back and forth to the teller, double-checking that I was boarding the correct bus. During this time, I had my first encounter with a homeless person who attempted to steal from me. Fortunately, a kind stranger intervened, shooing them away and advising me on how to identify potential threats, urging me to keep to myself and only engage with people in uniforms. I sat at the bus station for what felt like an eternity, waiting for the next bus. After three consecutive days of travel, hunger gnawing at me, and at that moment only twenty dollars left in my pocket, I desperately needed a shower. I had an additional $200 waiting for me at a Western Union in Georgia, but I had to reach there first. Finally, after hours of waiting and transferring between buses, I arrived in Georgia the following day at 6:00 PM. I was utterly exhausted! My host came to pick me up from the bus stop and drove me to his apartment. Although he offered a room, I couldn't sleep or shower. I urgently needed to buy toiletries, so we headed to the store. I managed to use that last twenty dollars, and then he took me to meet some Cameroonians in the city. Overwhelmed by fatigue, I ended up falling asleep for a few hours at someone's house. They kindly let me rest and woke me up when it was time to leave. The jet lag was intense. Finally, I had the opportunity to take a shower, and it felt like a long-awaited Christmas gift.

The place I grew up:

I was born in Douala, Cameroon, and spent my childhood in the small town of Manoka before eventually traveling to Europe for my studies. Cameroon, officially known as the Republic of Cameroon, is a country located in Central Africa. It is bordered by Nigeria to the west, Chad to the northeast, the Central African Republic to the east, Equatorial Guinea, Gabon, and the Republic of the Congo to the south, and the Atlantic Ocean to the southwest.

Cameroon is known for its diverse geography, which includes coastal plains, mountains, plateaus, and dense rainforests. The country is often referred to as "Africa in miniature" due to its wide range of landscapes and cultures.

The population of Cameroon is estimated to be over 26 million people, comprising various ethnic groups including the Bantu, Fulani, Bamileke, and many others. The official languages are English and French, reflecting the country's colonial history.

Cameroon has a rich cultural heritage with over 250 ethnic groups, each contributing to the country's vibrant traditions, music, dance, and cuisine. Traditional ceremonies and festivals are an integral part of Cameroonian life, showcasing the diversity and unity of its people.

The economy of Cameroon is also diverse, with sectors such as agriculture, oil and gas, mining, manufacturing, and services contributing to its GDP. The country is known for its agricultural products, including coffee, cocoa, bananas, and palm oil. It also has significant reserves of oil, natural gas, and minerals like bauxite and iron ore.

In terms of tourism, Cameroon is home to several national parks and wildlife reserves. At the Waza National Park and Korup National Park visitors can experience the beauty of Cameroon's flora and fauna. Mount Cameroon, the highest peak in West Africa, is a popular destination for hikers and climbers.

Overall, Cameroon is an exciting, fascinating country for both locals and tourists alike.

But not all locals.

Manoka, a town on an island also called Manoka, is home to a population where approximately half the residents live in poverty.

Manoka is known for its proximity to the Wouri River, which offers beautiful views and recreational opportunities. Visitors can take boat rides along the river, enjoying the scenic beauty and observing the daily activities of fishermen and traders, and its bustling markets.

When I first arrived in Manoka, there were a few beautiful houses, including my uncle's home and the house of my childhood best friend's father. These houses brought a glimmer of hope to our small town, and soon others began building more beautiful homes, elevating the value of the area.

However, what my uncle failed to realize was that the area was prone to flooding, and it wouldn't be long before we would be faced with the fear of drowning. Every rainy season, everyone would find themselves in danger due to rising floodwaters. I lost my birth certificate in one of these floods—a serious problem in a society that didn't have endless credit cards or qualifications to identify yourself. Despite the challenges, I was determined to go to school, often having to wade through the surging waters, sometimes even being carried by my uncle to reach the other side. There were moments when I would wake up to find water seeping into my bedroom. Thankfully, my uncle was always vigilant and would quickly shut down the electrical ports throughout the house. I shudder to think of the disaster we would have faced had he not taken those precautions.

Unfortunately, our luck took a turn for the worse when my uncle lost his job and we ran out of money. Dark days descended upon us, and we found ourselves going without food for days on end. It wasn't just us; the children in our neighborhood were also suffering from hunger. In response, we formed a group dedicated to providing meals for those in need. We pooled our resources, gathered food, and distributed it to those who required it the most. Within our group, we affectionately referred to each other as "Mola," a term that embodied the essence of friendship.

Meanwhile, my mother was far away in Europe, blissfully unaware of the hardships we were enduring back in Cameroon. She sent money to support me, but it always seemed to disappear into thin air, leaving us in the same dire circumstances. Growing up, I never knew or even met my father, and eventually I made the decision to stop pondering about him or seeking him out.

Every time I dared to ask about him, I was met with a deafening silence. It was only later, as I entered adulthood, that I mustered the courage to ask with more insistence, only to be informed of his passing.

My father:

The absence of my father has always cast a shadow over my life, and I have learned to come to terms with it. However, that doesn't mean I don't still yearn to know him, to understand who he was, and to experience his presence. I've heard whispers that I bear a striking resemblance to him and that I may have other siblings I know nothing about—I have two brothers in my life. It's disheartening to think that I may never have the chance to meet those others. You may wonder why I don't embark on a quest to find them. Well, Cameroon is not like the United States, and sometimes it's better to let sleeping dogs lie. I have found contentment and acceptance in my life and current circumstances in America.

I've heard tales of my father being a successful businessman. Perhaps that's where my entrepreneurial drive stems from? I consider myself incredibly fortunate to have my two amazing younger brothers, who have grown into exceptional men. I had the privilege of raising them for a while before my mother took over. That experience also profoundly shaped me, molding me into the woman and mother I am today.

My mother:

Now that I am a mother myself, I truly understand the immense struggles my own mother endured to raise us. I can now empathize with her distant gaze, lost in deep contemplation, as she tirelessly sought solutions to every challenge we faced. She was a pillar of strength, radiating beauty and embodying hard work. She possessed an uncanny intuition that guided her decisions. Like in many families, my mother and I often clashed, but our differences never hindered the love we had for each other. I hold an abiding respect for her, and I will forever miss her presence as I witness my own children blossom into remarkable adults. Our disagreements mostly stemmed from the fact that I always felt abandoned by her during the years I needed her most.

In the delicate years of my early childhood, when I was just a fragile three-year-old, my mother faced an agonizing decision. She entrusted me to the care of my uncle, as if I were his own flesh and blood. As time passed, I grew to accept that my mother had vanished from my life.

It wasn't until I reached the age of fifteen that I caught a fleeting glimpse of her again. She was not *gone*. Simply, she instead chose not to be *there*. My mother had gotten married and travelled to the United States where she gave birth to my two younger brothers.

In that poignant moment, I felt an overwhelming sense of exclusion, as if I was unwanted—and yes, abandoned. The years of longing for my mother's love had taken a toll on my young heart, leaving behind scars that seemed impossible to heal. I yearned for her warmth, her embrace, and the reassurance that only a mother could provide.

As I navigated through my teenage years, I found solace in the arms of my uncle, who had become a pillar of support in my life. He had taken on the role of both a father and a mother, showering me with love and care. Yet, deep down, I couldn't shake off the ache of not having my mother by my side.

With each passing day, I grew more determined and I reached out to her, hoping to rekindle the bond that had been lost for so long. Our interactions were awkward at first, filled with stilted conversations and forced smiles. As time went on, we began to find common ground, slowly building a fragile connection.

It was during one of our conversations that my mother revealed the reasons behind her leaving. She had faced her own battles, struggling with personal demons that had consumed her. Guilt washed over me as I realized that her absence had not been a choice, but a consequence of circumstances beyond her control.

In that moment, my heart softened, and I began to understand the complexities of life and that forgiveness was not only for her, but also for myself. I had carried the weight of resentment for far too long, and it was time to let go.

Over time, our relationship blossomed, and the void that had once seemed insurmountable began to fill. We shared laughter, tears, and the stories of our lives, slowly weaving the threads together again.

***

For years, I grappled with the harsh reality that parents often make sacrifices for the betterment of their children's future. It took me a considerable amount of time to come to terms with this truth, and I am genuinely grateful for the sacrifices my mother made to provide me with a better life. However, for a long period, being abandoned by my own mother caused me to retreat into the depths of my own self, always believing that people would inevitably leave, and that trust was an incredibly rare commodity.

This belief shaped my interactions with others, making it difficult for me to let anyone get too close. I built walls around my heart, shielding myself from the pain of potential rejection. It became a defense mechanism, a way to protect myself from the inevitable disappointment that seemed to follow me wherever I went.

As I grew older, I became fiercely independent, relying solely on myself for support and validation. I excelled academically, throwing myself into my studies as a means of distraction. I buried my emotions deep within, refusing to let them surface, afraid of the vulnerability they would bring.

But no matter how hard I tried to suppress my longing for a mother's love, it remained a constant ache in my heart. I yearned for the warmth of her embrace, the sound of her voice whispering words of comfort and encouragement. I longed for the feeling of belonging, of being unconditionally loved and accepted.

In my quest for self-discovery, I immersed myself in literature, finding solace in the stories of others who had experienced similar struggles. And through it all, I slowly began to understand that I had the power to rewrite my own narrative.

And slowly, ever so slowly, I started to let go of the fears, and I learned that my worth was not defined by the actions of others, but by the love and strength I carried within myself. I could create my own sense of belonging, and I didn't need to rely on anyone else to feel whole.

Today, I am no longer the fragile three-year-old or the lost fifteen-year-old. I am a survivor, a warrior who has emerged from the depths of despair stronger and more resilient than ever before. As I continue to navigate this vast world, I do so with a newfound sense of hope and a belief that love and connection are not only possible but also worth fighting for.

The loss of my mother:

After the joy of rebuilding our relationship, the loss of my mother to liver cancer was devastating. The years leading up to her diagnosis were filled with frustration and helplessness as doctors continuously misdiagnosed her stomach pain as heartburn. I would spend countless hours at the pharmacy, picking up heartburn medication that provided no relief for her. It was heartbreaking to see my mother curled up in bed, crying in agony, while I stood by feeling utterly powerless.

With the responsibilities of raising my own children and working a job, it became increasingly difficult to attend to my mother's needs. We were in Massachusetts, and I made the difficult decision to ask her to stay with my brothers in Georgia, believing that they would be better equipped to cope. Little did I know that her stomach pain was a symptom of something far more sinister—cancer. It was only when she was hospitalized for months that her late-stage diagnosis was finally discovered.

During this time, my brother Felix took on the role of caring for our mother, accompanying her to the hospital and chemotherapy sessions. Unfortunately, now I couldn't be there for her as I was in the later stages of pregnancy. Traveling to Georgia was not feasible, and my mother, always selfless, insisted that I stay put until after I had given birth. She had hoped to be present in the delivery room, just as she had been for my other two children, but her illness robbed her of that.

Despite the physical distance, I made sure to speak with my mother daily, listening to her pain-filled voice and feeling completely helpless. It wasn't until after giving birth to her last grandchild that I finally had the chance to visit her. The vibrant and strong woman I had known had been reduced to a frail figure, barely able to stand. Yet, my mother mustered the strength to join me for a meal at a restaurant, cradling her grandchild and blessing her with tears in her eyes. It was during this bittersweet moment that I suspected it would be the last time I would see her, that time was running out.

With a heavy heart, I flew back home to Massachusetts. A few days later, I received the devastating news that she was already nearing the end of her journey and that I needed to return to say my final goodbyes. This time, I brought all my children with me, wanting them to have the chance to bid farewell to their beloved grandmother. When we left her side, she was still clinging to life.

Days after my return, I had a dream that my mother had miraculously recovered. In the dream, she turned her back to me, picking something up from the ground, and assured me that she was okay. It brought a sense of relief, a glimmer of hope that she would be alright. Little did I know that this dream was her way of saying goodbye to me.

Two days later, I received a call from my brother Andre, informing me of my mother's passing. I was frozen, unable to move or leave my bed for days. The pain was unbearable, and it felt as though the world had come crashing down around me. I couldn't eat, but I had to find the strength to feed my baby and take care of my other children.

In the midst of my grief, Pastor Mary came to my home with food for the kids and offered her prayers and support. She encouraged me to eat something, reminding me of the importance of taking care of myself for the sake of my baby.

The pain of losing my mother remains with me to this day, a constant ache in my heart that I struggle to overcome. But I know now, as I knew back then, that I must find the strength to carry on, for my children and for the memory of the incredible woman who brought me into this world.

My grandmother:

My grandmother Sophie was a remarkable woman who played a significant role in shaping my upbringing. I first met her when I was just seven years old, and she was already battling illness.

That summer, I was sent to stay with my grandmother, and it was during that time that I also had the opportunity to meet my great grandmother. My great grandmother was a complex individual, often feared by many. I witnessed countless arguments between her and my grandmother, but beneath their fierce disagreements there was an undeniable love.

For some years afterwards, every summer I would pack my bags and eagerly head to the village where my grandmother lived. Life in the village was a true delight for me. I developed a deep love for nature. I relished the time spent on the farm, but I must admit that cooking was not initially something I enjoyed. It felt like a chore, until my grandmother began to show me the true beauty of cooking—how it could be both a skill and an art form.

After my great grandmother passed away, my grandmother needed me in the village more than ever. I was the only grandchild who enjoyed the idea of working on the farm, while the rest of my cousins preferred a different path. My grandmother became my greatest teacher, imparting wisdom about life, people, and the world in general. She taught me the importance of cooking and cleaning, instilling in me a sense of responsibility and the significance of these tasks.

Moreover, my grandmother taught me what it meant to be a woman and how to navigate society with grace and dignity. She emphasized the importance of strength, urging me to never fear hardship or hard work, but rather to regard them as steppingstones towards a better life. She encouraged me to never give up on my dreams and to always pursue what I believed in.

Every time I step into the kitchen now, I can feel her presence, guiding my hands and whispering her secret recipes in my ear. Her passion for food is her legacy that I strive to honor with every dish I create.

Mola Foods, my business, was born out of a desire to share the flavors and traditions that my grandmother instilled in me. From her homemade sauces to her unique spice blends, I have carefully crafted each product to capture the essence of her cooking. It brings me immense joy to see customers savoring the same flavors that once graced our family table.

My connection to my grandmother's teachings doesn't end there. Jals cuisine Bantu, my restaurant, is a tribute to her culinary expertise. Inspired by the vibrant and diverse flavors of Bantu cuisine, I have combined her traditional recipes with my own creative twists. Every dish that leaves my kitchen is a testament to her influence and a reflection of the love and passion she poured into her cooking.

As I continue to grow both Mola Foods and Jals cuisine

Bantu, I am reminded of the invaluable lessons my grandmother taught me. She taught me the importance of using fresh, high-quality ingredients, the art of balancing flavors, and the significance of cooking with love. These teachings have become the foundation of my business, guiding me through every decision and inspiring me to constantly innovate and improve.

Though my grandmother may no longer be physically present, her spirit lives on through the delicious creations that bear her influence. I am forever grateful for the time I had with her, for the memories we shared in the kitchen, and for the wisdom she imparted upon me.

My grandmother's guidance and love also helped shape me into the person I am today. I am forever grateful for the time I spent with her in the village so long ago, for the knowledge she imparted, and for the unwavering support she provided. My grandmother Sophie will always hold a special place in my heart, and her teachings will continue to guide me.

My uncle:

At my mother's desperate insistence, my uncle took on the responsibility of caring for me when I was just three years old. His then-wife, Brigid played the role of a mother figure in my life for fifteen years on and off as I was sent to different homes depending on who needed me to go help them with their children. She was a kind and loving woman who faced the heartbreaking challenge of not being able to have children of her own, something which caused ongoing struggles in their marriage.

My uncle had his own flaws, such as battling alcoholism and seeking attention, and he had once lived a prosperous life. Circumstances changed when his job either relocated to another country or his contract ended, leaving him without any financial stability. His only skill seemed to be selling sand and stones, and when he couldn't find similar work, he lacked the motivation to explore other options. Consequently, he resorted to continuing his sand and stone business independently.

I grew up in a tumultuous environment, constantly surrounded by chaos and violence. Witnessing my uncle's destructive behavior and the abuse inflicted upon his wife and sisters left a lasting impact on me. The memories of that fateful day when he almost took his sister's life with a knife still haunt me to this day.

Brigid showered me with love and care. However, my uncle's alcoholism and reckless behavior overshadowed any sense of stability or security. He lived on the edge, constantly seeking thrills and indulging in vices. His financial downfall only exacerbated his destructive tendencies, as he would make money one day and squander it all on his addictions the next.

I watched as he spiraled deeper into his self-destructive patterns. His entitlement and expectation of some sort of repayment for caring for me made me feel I was trapped and indebted. There was no gratitude or acknowledgment for the sacrifices *we* all made on his behalf, including the support my mother had provided for years.

After my mother's untimely passing, my uncle's true colors emerged. In a bid to claim a piece of land that rightfully belonged to my mother and the rest of the family, he denied my existence, stating that she had left no children behind. It was a betrayal that cut deep.

I found myself longing for a sense of normalcy. Today, the scars may still linger, but I am forever determined to rise above the darkness and create a better future for myself and my children.

My children:

Children are a precious blessing bestowed upon us by a higher power. I have been truly blessed by the Lord with three extraordinary gifts. However, raising children is no easy task. There is no instruction manual or guide to follow; you simply have to navigate through it as best as you can. The challenges become even more daunting when you are a single parent. No one warns you about the sleepless nights or the unexpected difficulties that arise when you are solely responsible for raising a child. No one prepares you for the countless needs you must fulfill or the fires you must extinguish along the way.

Furthermore, no one adequately prepares you for the growth and development of your child, and the sacrifices you must make to ensure their well-being, protection, and provision. No one warns you about the lack of respect and sense of entitlement that can arise as they begin to believe they are grown, despite still depending on you. In America, children are often led to believe they are more mature than they truly are.

As parents, we all desire for our children to succeed and surpass our own achievements, ultimately becoming responsible adults, at the same being often clueless about how their individual journeys will unfold. I consider myself fortunate to have been blessed with good-hearted children. God has gifted them with a compassionate nature, making it easier for me to raise them alone without feeling overwhelmed. Despite the challenges, we have formed a close-knit bond as a family.

As my children grow older, I am constantly reminded of the importance of instilling values and traditions in their lives. I have always emphasized the significance of loving one another and treating others with kindness and respect. It warms my heart to see them embracing these teachings and carrying them forward.

Through the challenges of being a single parent, I have strived to provide a stable and nurturing environment. I have worked hard to shield them from my own struggles and ensure that they feel safe and loved. However, children are perceptive, and they have a way of sensing when something is amiss. They have shown incredible empathy and understanding, offering their support and love in return.

As they continue on their life journey, I hope that my children will remain close-knit. I pray that they will always be there for one another, supporting and uplifting each other through life's ups and downs. I have witnessed the bond they share, and it fills me with immense joy and gratitude.

I also hope that they will carry forward the traditions and values I have imparted in them. These teachings have shaped their character and guided their decisions, and I believe they will continue to do so in the future. I have taught them the importance of not only loving one another but also extending that love to their neighbors. I hope they will always have open hearts and be willing to lend a helping hand to those in need.

As a parent, I am aware that I cannot control every aspect of my children's lives. They will face their own challenges and make their own choices. But I am confident that the foundation I have laid for them will serve as a compass, guiding them towards becoming responsible and compassionate adults.

Quite simply, I am grateful for the gift of my children. They have brought immeasurable joy and purpose into my life.

Giving my life to Jesus Christ:

During my upbringing, I faced immense despair, attempting to end my life not once, but twice. It was during my last attempt that something extraordinary happened. A gentle voice called out to me, urging me to confide in it, assuring me that I was cherished and valued. This voice, filled with compassion, proclaimed that I was intelligent, talented, and deserving. Initially, I dismissed it as a figment of my imagination, desperately trying to silence it. The voice persisted, growing louder and more insistent, until it implored me to reach for my Bible and pray.

Overwhelmed with emotion, I fell to my knees and pleaded with God for forgiveness, vowing to banish any thoughts of self-harm. With trembling hands, I opened the Bible and began to read. Tears streamed down my face as I experienced a profound sense of salvation that day. The love I felt from God was enough to dispel any lingering thoughts of despair.

I was fifteen years old, and I was saved by the boundless grace of God. From that moment on, my spirituality flourished, and I found solace in the pages of the Bible, alternating between tears and laughter as I delved into its teachings.

A surge of joy, love, and bravery engulfed me in an instant. It was during that fateful night that I saw the immense power of divinity, for only God could possess such strength. So, I embarked on a path of humility and compassion.

As I grew in my faith in God and experienced His love and grace in my life, I felt a longing to surrender my heart completely to Him. My life had been missing something, and I yearned for a real connection with my Creator.

One day, as I immersed myself in prayer and reflection, I felt an overwhelming sense of peace and clarity wash over me. It was in that moment that I knew I was ready to give my life to Christ. With a humble heart and a renewed spirit, I made the decision to invite Jesus into my life as my Lord and Savior.

From that day forward, my journey with Christ began. I sought to understand His teachings, to live according to His word, and to follow His example of love, compassion, and forgiveness. As I delved into the Scriptures, I discovered the incredible depth of God's love for me and for all of humanity.

With each passing day, my relationship with Christ grew stronger. I found solace in His presence, guidance in His wisdom, and strength in His promises. Through the ups and downs of life, I learned to lean on Him, trusting that He would never leave me nor forsake me.

As I walked this path of faith, I encountered challenges and obstacles that tested my commitment. Yet, through it all, I experienced the transformative power of God's grace. He lifted me up when I stumbled, forgave me when I faltered, and filled my heart with purpose and joy.

My decision to give my life to Christ was not a one-time event but rather the beginning of a lifelong journey. It has sharpened my perspective, influenced my choices, and transformed my character. I strive to live a life that reflects His love, sharing His message of hope and redemption with those around me.

In surrendering my life to Christ, I have found a deep and abiding peace that surpasses all understanding. I am grateful for the unending grace and mercy He extends to me, and I am humbled by the privilege of being called His child. My faith in God continues to grow, and I am forever grateful for the day I made the decision to give my life to Christ.

Thriving in the face of adversity. Embracing resilience in a life of scarcity:

There were countless occasions when our home lacked sustenance, leaving us famished for days on end. However, Brigid would always manage to secure bread and beignets, ensuring that my cousin and I had at least one meal a day. To combat the pangs of hunger, we sought solace in sleep. Our household was plagued by many days filled with hunger, fear, and despair. It was a place where my uncle would subject his wife to brutal beatings, inflicting wounds upon her eyes and lips, yet she remained steadfastly loyal to him. As the saying goes, "in suffering and happiness till death do us part." He would return home intoxicated, seeking confrontation with his wife, his sisters, and nearly everyone else in the house—except for me. I was his cherished favorite, and he shielded me from harm. Even so, my uncle's violent outbursts, triggered by the simplest of questions, were too much for me to bear. I began to question the sanctity of marriage, pondering alternative methods of raising children, and contemplating the true purpose of motherhood.

Witnessing such heartless behavior left me scarred and shook me to my core, and I made a solemn promise to myself. No man would ever have the power to hurt me, physically or emotionally. I refused to ever subject myself to an abusive relationship, even though admittedly I *had* unknowingly endured an emotionally abusive marriage before finding the strength to leave.

Despite this resolve, so many of my life decisions were driven by a desperate search for love in all the wrong places. Growing up without a father, I mistakenly sought to fill it by becoming attached too quickly to others. I yearned for validation and someone to prove that I mattered. It took numerous failed attempts at love for me to see that I didn't need a man to validate my worth. I didn't need to be dependent on others. What I truly needed was to cultivate self-love and self-acceptance.

Resilience was a quality I possessed, but self-love was something I lacked. It was only after enduring a failed marriage and several unsuccessful relationships that I finally took a long, hard look at myself. I questioned what was wrong with *me* and what I was doing wrong in my pursuit of love.

The answer came—I needed to prioritize self-love above all else.

There was nothing inherently wrong with me. I had simply fallen for partners who failed to appreciate what they had. I had been settling for less and tolerating more than I deserved, all because of my desperate longing for love, regardless of who it came from.

I decided to focus on personal growth and let go of the

relationships that were holding me back. I cleared my path and immediately felt a sense of relief. It dawned on me that my children needed to witness me as a role model, and I couldn't fulfill that role if I continued to neglect my own self-love and rely on others for validation. I had to prioritize loving myself first, even if it meant being selfish. Although it was a bittersweet process, as I let go of long-held insecurities and emotional baggage, each passing day brought me closer to a newfound sense of empowerment. I discovered my voice and learned to stand up for myself, unafraid of gossip or judgment. I firmly held my ground and disrupted the status quo. I claimed my space and made it known that I existed. I confidently rejected one-sided relationships and embraced the idea of being alone. For the first time, I no longer felt the need for a man to be a part of my life. A man was no longer a necessity; I had become whole on my own.

I had viewed a man as the missing piece to complete my life's intricate puzzle. This puzzle piece had to seamlessly fit into my existence, complementing every aspect of it. I yearned for a partner who would not only be my companion and lover but also someone who would value my time and treat me with utmost respect. I longed for a man who would treat me like royalty, like the queen that I am. Until that fateful moment when this extraordinary man enters my life, I will continue to accept the joys of life, cherishing myself, nurturing my own well-being, and raising my beloved children. Life holds immense promise, and I find myself truly content in my own element.

Motherhood and dating:

As a mother, I am plagued by daily fears for the welfare of my children and myself. This fear has led me to be extremely cautious and selective when it comes to introducing potential partners to my children. I have learned to trust my instincts and take things slow, prioritizing the safety and well-being of my little ones above all else.

But even with all the precautions, there is always a lingering doubt in the back of my mind. Will this person truly care for my children as their own? Will they be a positive influence and role model? These questions constantly weigh on my heart, making it difficult to fully let my guard down in any new relationship.

I have seen too many stories of single mothers who have been deceived and hurt by individuals who seemed genuine at first. It's a painful reminder that not everyone has the best intentions, especially when it comes to vulnerable children. This knowledge has made me fiercely protective, always on high alert for any signs of potential danger.

Yet, despite the challenges and fears, I refuse to let them consume me.

Instead, I am determined to find love and companionship, not just for myself but also for the sake of my children. Their lives will be enriched to see their mother happy and fulfilled, to witness a healthy and loving relationship firsthand.

So, I continue to navigate the world of dating with caution, but also with hope. I have learned to trust my instincts, to listen to that inner voice that tells me whether someone is genuine or not. I have also surrounded myself with a strong support system of friends and family who have my back and will help me make the best decisions.

In the end, I know that I cannot control everything, and there will always be an element of uncertainty. But I refuse to let fear dictate my life. And in the process, I hope to find a partner who will join me in this journey, someone who will love and cherish my children as much as I do.

We can never be certain if someone is genuinely good or if they will inflict irreparable harm upon our precious ones. People can change in an instant, becoming a shocking stranger you've never seen before. This unfortunate reality extends beyond single mothers and also affects married couples, including fathers and stepfathers. It's a sickening and twisted truth that we may not want to acknowledge, but child molesters often lurk within our closest circles. They can be uncles, boyfriends, brothers, sisters, mothers or even the child's own father. Yes, outsiders can pose a threat, but the most horrifying instances occur within the confines of our own homes.

So, how do we confront these nightmarish situations? What do we do when our child comes to us in the middle of the night, sobbing and uttering those heart-wrenching words, "He did it again, Mom. This time, I couldn't keep it to myself. He did it again."

How can we possibly help our child and ourselves navigate the excruciating pain and suffering, knowing that the scars may never fully heal?

I, too, at nine and fourteen years old experienced those haunting moments, but I was trapped in a world where silence reigned supreme. There was no one to confide in, no safe haven for my pain. The shame that enveloped me dictated that I keep my suffering hidden, leaving me to endure the agony by myself. I was utterly alone, unable to share my burden with a single soul.

My untold adult incident:

I vividly recall a distressing incident from my own past. At the age of fourteen, I visited my best friend's house, only to find her father there while she was out running errands with her mother. Since he was my aunt's ex-husband and the father of my cousin, I felt at ease waiting for my friend. Little did I know that this man, who had been hiding his predatory nature, would soon reveal his true colors. Slowly, he began caressing my legs, his hands inching their way up to my thighs. I was paralyzed with fear and panic. My heart raced, and my palms grew clammy. Desperate to escape, I mustered the courage to ask for a glass of water, hoping it would provide a momentary distraction and allow me to flee. Fortunately, my cousin unexpectedly arrived and informed me that his sister wouldn't be home until the following day. I had been deceived by my friend's father.

Seizing the opportunity, I bolted out of the house as fast as my legs could carry me. I never looked back. From that day forward, I made excuses to avoid returning to that house. Even when I encountered him on the streets, and he would invite me to stop by to "see my best friend", I steadfastly refused. I was one of the fortunate ones, but not all children are as lucky.

The pain and trauma inflicted upon innocent children can leave lasting scars that may never fully fade away. As parents, it is our duty to support and guide our children through these unimaginable hardships. We must create a safe space for them to express their emotions, ensuring they know they are not alone in their suffering. Seeking professional help, such as therapy or counseling, can provide invaluable support for both the child and ourselves as we navigate this painful journey.

It is crucial to educate ourselves and our children about personal boundaries, consent, and the importance of speaking up when something feels wrong. By fostering open and honest communication, we empower our children to trust their instincts and confide in us when they encounter any form of abuse or exploitation.

As we embark on this arduous path, we must remember that healing takes time. It is a gradual process that requires patience, understanding, and unwavering love. Together, we can help our children reclaim their lives and find solace amidst the darkness.

My previous encounter was with a relative of my uncle when I was only nine years old. On a late evening, my uncle asked his cousin to accompany me to fetch a beer. In Cameroon, in my time period, it was common for a child to go buy beer late at night for family members. Bars where very close to our home. As we ventured through a dimly lit alley, he abruptly halted, exposing himself and demanding that I perform a degrading act. Overwhelmed with shock, I sprinted away, seeking refuge in my home by climbing through a window. The experience left me physically ill, confined to my bed for three agonizing days, plagued by nausea and fever. The confusion, fear, and shame prevented me from confiding in anyone about these disturbing incidents. It was a perplexing time as I struggled to comprehend why such horrors were befalling me.

These traumatic events resulted in making me a fiercely protective mother. I have made it a priority to establish open lines of communication with my children, urging them to confide in me about every aspect of their lives, both positive and negative. I want them to feel safe and unafraid to share their experiences. Safeguarding my children has become my mission, constantly vigilant and cautious about allowing others to get too close. This has made *my* dating a challenging endeavor, as I am perpetually haunted by the "what-ifs."

But living in constant fear is detrimental to our well-being. Life is too fleeting to be consumed by apprehension. It is imperative that we unite and devise effective strategies to combat these fears, reclaim our lives, and foster a harmonious world where everyone can coexist peacefully.

Sometimes, I understand, this requires giving people the benefit of the doubt.

I have been blessed with incredible children and opportunities in life. During our youth, we often fall in love, believing that our affections are reciprocated and that we will be treated with kindness. Sometimes, we mistake intense passion for genuine love, and pleasure for a deep connection. We meet individuals and automatically assume they are wonderful, trustworthy people.

Often this is true. Sometimes, it is not.

My marriage:

During my youthful days, I held grand visions of matrimony and discovering a companion who would wholeheartedly uplift me in my professional endeavors and aspirations. Since childhood, I have possessed an unwavering ambition, ceaselessly pursuing triumph in every facet of existence—be it my career, my loved ones, or my abode. I would often imagine encountering my knight in shining armor, gallantly riding atop a majestic white steed, and embarking on a lifelong journey of bliss. Alas, little did I comprehend that reality frequently veers away from the path of our dreams.

As I grew older, I realized that finding true love and a fulfilling partnership is not as simple as fairy tales make it out to be. Relationships require effort, compromise, and a deep understanding of one another. The path to finding my perfect match was filled with ups and downs, heartbreaks, and lessons learned.

I soon discovered that my career aspirations and personal goals were not always aligned with those of potential partners. Some were intimidated by my drive and ambition, while others simply couldn't comprehend the amount of dedication I put into my work. It became clear that finding someone who would truly support me was no easy task.

While reality may have diverged from my childhood dreams, I now understand that true happiness lies in finding someone who complements and enhances my journey rather than completing it. Marriage and partnership are not about finding someone to fulfill all our dreams, but rather about embarking on a shared adventure, facing life's challenges together, and celebrating each other's successes. And though the path to finding love and support may not always be straightforward, the journey is undoubtedly worth it when you find someone who believes in you as much as you believe in yourself.

Fortunately, I have been blessed with the presence of extraordinary individuals who have not only believed in me but also inspired me to remain authentic to myself and my aspirations. I have always possessed an unwavering clarity about what I truly wanted and needed from life. However, the course of my existence took an unexpected turn when I encountered an individual who, unbeknownst to me, concealed a malevolent nature beneath a captivating facade. Initially, this person exuded charm and warmth, effortlessly captivating my heart. Despite a persistent inner voice urging caution and resistance against temptation, I chose to follow the desires of my heart instead. I was cognizant of the deceit, yet I deliberately chose to overlook it. My friends and even my mother saw through the veil of deception and warned me, but I obstinately disregarded their concerns.

As time went on, the cracks in his charming facade began to show. He became possessive and controlling, manipulating me into believing that his actions were out of love and concern. Slowly, he isolated me from my friends and family, making me believe that he was the only one who truly understood and cared for me.

I found myself trapped in a toxic relationship, constantly walking on eggshells and living in fear of his unpredictable moods. My dreams and aspirations took a backseat as I struggled to keep the peace and appease him. The once vibrant and ambitious person I used to be was slowly fading away, replaced by a shell of my former self.

It took a moment of clarity, a glimmer of the person I used to be, to realize that I deserved better. I deserved a companion who was on my side, not tear me down and hold me back. With newfound strength and determination, I made the difficult decision to break free from his grasp.

It wasn't easy. Leaving behind someone who had become such a significant part of my life was painful and terrifying. But I knew deep down that it was the right choice for my well-being and happiness. I sought support from my loved ones, who had been patiently waiting for me to come to my senses. They welcomed me with open arms, reminding me of my worth and helping me rebuild the shattered pieces of my self-esteem.

In the aftermath of that toxic relationship, I learned valuable lessons about the importance of self-love and self-respect. I vowed to never again settle for anything less than what I deserved. I rekindled my passion for my dreams and aspirations, determined to make up for lost time and reclaim my sense of purpose.

While the scars may never fully fade, they serve as a constant reminder of my strength and resilience. I am no longer that naive and vulnerable person. I have emerged from the darkness with a newfound wisdom and a renewed sense of self.

As I continue on, I remain cautious but hopeful. I know that not every encounter will be tainted by deception and betrayal. I have learned to trust my instincts and surround myself with genuine friends.

Never before had I experienced such a profound and consuming love as I did for this enigmatic figure. Little did I know that I was being ensnared in a web of deceit and subjected to emotional and, at times, physical torment. Yet, I clung to the hope that beneath his devilish exterior, there lay a glimmer of goodness. I yearned for him to recognize my inherent value and to reciprocate the love and respect I so desperately craved. I fabricated excuses for his abhorrent behavior, repeatedly allowing him back into my life despite my initial resolve to break free. And then, unexpected news shattered my world—I was pregnant.

The revelation left me utterly bewildered, for I had been meticulous in taking my birth control pills. How could this be happening? The timing was far from ideal, as I had just embarked on my career and had aspirations of completing my education before considering motherhood.

I wasn't at all prepared to become a mother at that moment.

Oh, how I questioned the timing of it all, but deep down, I felt a glimmer of joy knowing that I would soon bring a precious child into this world. However, I couldn't ignore the fact that I was entangled with someone who seemed to embody the devil himself. Fear consumed me as I pondered the consequences of my actions while dealing with the man who would become the father of my child. The weight of it all left me trembling and drenched in night sweats.

To my astonishment, when I mustered the courage to share the news of my pregnancy, his response was far from supportive. He accused me of ruining his life by bringing children into it and vowed to retaliate by ruining mine. Throughout my pregnancy, I found myself burdened with an overwhelming amount of stress. It became clear that I needed to distance myself from the toxic situation, if only for a while. Thankfully, my friends became my pillars of strength, faithfully visiting me every Saturday to ensure I never felt alone. My brother, too, became my biggest cheerleader, offering guidance and companionship. Despite the turmoil caused by the one who now claims to be a proud father, I was surrounded by love and experienced a beautiful pregnancy.

Looking back, I can't help but admit my own foolishness. I was naive to believe that the person standing before me, uttering words of love, had entered my life with pure intentions. Despite the warnings and the signs I chose to ignore, I was unwilling to see the truth that others saw so clearly. Love truly can blind us, especially when we allow our hearts instead of our minds to lead us. I found myself trapped without seeing it coming, completely unaware of the manipulative games the devil was playing. He denied his own child, only to later demand a place in their life. He foolishly believed that they were the reason he couldn't afford another luxury car, and he made it clear that they were not welcome in his world.

The abuse:

As a person facing immense challenges, I found myself in a situation where I had to confront my worst fears once again. This time, it felt like I was living with a malevolent force, a true embodiment of my nightmares. Here I was in an unhealthy marriage, with two small children, and I was constantly marginalized and subjected to taunts due to my African heritage and humble background. Words like "gold digger," "ignorant," "stupid," and "unworthy" were thrown at me, yet I stayed because I held onto my misguided principles. I believed that my children deserved to be raised by both parents under one roof, even if it meant enduring unbearable consequences.

I prioritized my children's happiness above all else, even if it meant enduring a lesser treatment and remaining in an abusive relationship. I believed that providing a stable upbringing and the opportunity to be raised by both parents was worth the pain I was enduring. I held onto the belief in the sanctity of marriage, no matter the circumstances. However, I now acknowledge that at the very start I placed my trust and belief in the wrong person, the wrong man.

One day it struck me that I, too, was someone's child, and my death would inflict genuine grief upon those who cared for me. This revelation caused a shift in my perspective, and I began to see life through a different lens. Then I caught a glimpse of my frail reflection in a mirror, and I crumbled to my knees, overwhelmed by tears. Exhaustion consumed me, and I found solace in tearful slumber. The weight of my responsibilities as a new mother to my second child, coupled with the challenges of breastfeeding, had taken a toll on my mental well-being.

I was battling depression, and it was time to seek help and make a change.

Seeking help, I visited my doctor who prescribed medication as a solution. I found myself hesitant to take the pills. As I held the bottle in my hands, conflicting thoughts swirled in my mind. Surrendering to depression seemed like the only option if I were to consume the medication. But deep down, I knew there had to be another way.

With a fierce determination burning within me, I made a resolute decision to take charge of my own well-being. I sought refuge in a gym, finding solace and strength through physical activity as I fought the shadows that consumed me. Simultaneously, I turned to the pages of my Bible, pouring out my heart to the Divine, seeking guidance in my darkest moments. Miraculously, I emerged victorious over postpartum depression, defying the odds without the aid of medication.

It's crucial to emphasize that not everyone possesses the same resilience and ability to overcome postpartum depression in this way. For some, medication becomes an essential lifeline, providing the necessary support to function and heal. My personal beliefs regarding medication differ, as I am hesitant to rely on pharmaceuticals. Instead, I strive to explore alternative avenues of coping and healing, reserving medication as a last resort when all other options have been exhausted.

Reflecting upon the principles I had set for my life, I admitted to the mistakes I had made. Now that I had children, their well-being became my priority. Even if it meant becoming a single mother and raising them alone, I knew I had to create a healthy environment for their upbringing.

With unwavering determination, I gathered our belongings and made the decision to leave. This time, I took the necessary steps to file for divorce, knowing there was no turning back. I landed in Massachusetts and never went back. I don't wish divorce on anyone—it was the worse period of my life. The entire process was emotionally draining, filled with endless arguments, and bitter disputes.

I had entered into the divorce proceedings with the hope of a fair and amicable resolution. It quickly became apparent that my ex-spouse's lawyer was more interested in prolonging the process and escalating tensions than finding a mutually beneficial solution. It seemed as though they were intentionally stoking the flames of conflict, pushing us further apart rather than helping us find common ground.

As the days turned into weeks and the weeks into months, I was drowning in legal fees that seemed to skyrocket with each passing day. It was disheartening to witness the exorbitant charges for every phone call, email, or even a simple consultation. It became evident that some lawyers were more interested in maximizing their profits than providing genuine support and guidance.

The experience left me disillusioned and skeptical of the legal system. I couldn't help but wonder how many others had fallen victim to these unscrupulous practices. It was a stark reminder that not all lawyers are created equal, and finding one who genuinely cares about your best interests can be an arduous task.

Amidst the darkness, I also encountered a glimmer of hope. I stumbled upon a compassionate and ethical lawyer who restored my faith in the profession. They listened attentively, empathized with my situation, and worked tirelessly to ensure a fair settlement. Their dedication and commitment to my well-being were evident in every step of the process.

Through this experience, I learned the importance of thorough research and seeking recommendations when choosing legal representation. It is crucial to find a lawyer who not only possesses the necessary expertise but also demonstrates integrity and a genuine concern for their clients. Trusting someone with such a significant aspect of your life requires careful consideration and due diligence.

My divorce was undoubtedly a painful chapter in my life, and it also served as a valuable lesson. It taught me to be cautious, to advocate for myself, and to never settle for anything less than the best legal representation. Divorce is already a challenging and emotionally charged process, and having a lawyer who truly has your best interests at heart can make all the difference in the world.

Displaced life:

During my childhood, I experienced a constant cycle of moving from one house to another. For a period, I was in the care of one of my mother's sisters. This aunt subjected me to physical abuse, leaving me with permanent scars on my eyelid, face, and body. The severity of her actions even endangered my eyesight when she threw a bottle at my face. Filled with fear, I fled her house and embarked on a three-hour journey by foot to my uncle's place, blood streaming down my face. I only returned to her house to retrieve my belongings, vowing never to go back.

Within her home, I was akin to a modern-day Cinderella. My days were consumed by cooking, cleaning, and washing her baby's clothes, with no opportunity for anything else. Neglected academically, I fell behind in school, and my aunt displayed no concern for my well-being. I felt like an abandoned child, constantly being used by those around me for their own convenience. Eventually, I found myself living with another aunt whose husband took it upon himself to shave my hair. His reasoning was that I had more hair than his own daughters, and he wanted us all to be on equal footing. In this household, we were only provided with one meal a day and were forbidden from venturing outside. The lack of stability and constantly changing schools became the norm for me, as I was always thrust into new environments.

Returning to my alcoholic uncle's care seemed like a better solution, but it didn't last. The abuse he inflicted upon his own family became unbearable, and I finally mustered the courage to stand up to him. In response, he came after me, fueling my determination to escape. Fleeing with every ounce of strength I possessed, I nearly stumbled and fell face-first onto a fence adorned with broken glass. The sound of people's horrified screams filled the air, as they believed I had met my demise. Miraculously, I managed to leap over the fence, and the subsequent cries I heard were not of sorrow, but of joy. And then, there was a sound of something falling.

It was my uncle who had taken a fall. Desperate for help, I made a journey of four long hours by foot to reach my aunt, a skilled nurse practitioner. Exhausted and overwhelmed, I collapsed at her feet, slipping into a deep coma that lasted for three agonizing days. When I finally regained consciousness, the trauma of the experience still clung to me, leaving me unsettled and disoriented.

In the aftermath, I distanced myself from my uncle's house, avoiding it for years. Even with my mother's return, things did not improve. It was a peculiar existence, feeling like an orphan within my own family, as if I were a foster child. The sense of not belonging, of being out of place, weighed heavily upon me.

I began silently suffering whatever was thrown my way without uttering a single complaint. I endured, clinging to the hope that God held the answers I sought. Each night, tears streamed down my face as I questioned my purpose on this earth, wondering why I even existed. Eventually, I made a decision to wear a smile, regardless of the circumstances, and to maintain a positive outlook. I believed that if I constantly reminded myself of my worth and the fact that I was here for a reason, everything would eventually be alright. I knew deep within that I possessed the strength to survive any hardship that came my way.

I refused to let my past define me. I channeled my pain into motivation, vowing to create a better future for myself. I learned the power of resilience and the importance of finding strength in the darkest of times. I used the scars on my body as a reminder of the battles I had fought and the strength I had gained.

Today, I stand tall as a survivor, a testament to the human spirit's ability to overcome even the most unimaginable hardships. I continue to fight for justice and raise awareness about the lasting effects of abuse.

A look back:

Moving to the United States held the promise of a brighter future for both myself and my family in Cameroon, including my beloved grandmother, uncle, and others. I felt an immense responsibility to succeed in order to repay them for their sacrifices and the meager resources they had provided. However, the USA came with its own set of obstacles. I had never encountered racism before. Yet, everything changed the moment I set foot in America. It was a culture shock that opened my eyes to a new reality. What surprised me the most was the unexpected coldness I received from fellow black Americans.

As I began forming friendships within the African American community, I became aware of the deep divide that exists between Africans and African Americans. This division stems from a sense of abandonment felt by African Americans, as they believe that Africa turned its back on them during the painful era of slavery, which remains a significant factor contributing to this divide. It is truly unfortunate, as Africans view black Americans as an integral part of our cultural heritage, and we should actively seek to understand their roots and encourage them to explore the land from which their ancestors were forcibly taken. I am grateful to be raising my children in a country that offers abundant opportunities, and I consider myself fortunate to be a part of such a diverse group of people and a nation.

I have come to believe that my past mistakes and encounters with insincere individuals were not entirely in vain. They have taught me valuable lessons about trust, intuition, and the importance of self-reflection. I have learned to be more discerning and cautious when it comes to choosing the people I allow into my life.

While it is easy to blame others for their deceitful actions, holding onto resentment and anger only hinders my own growth. Instead, I choose to take responsibility for my own choices and actions. It is through this self-accountability that I can truly learn from my past and avoid repeating the same mistakes.

Letting go of my desperate desire for a life partner and the idea of remarriage was not an easy decision, but it was a necessary one. My happiness should not solely depend on finding someone to share my life with. I needed to find fulfillment within myself and focus on the things that truly brought me joy.

Shifting my focus towards my children and my career has been transformative. I have found immense happiness in being present for my children, witnessing their growth, and providing them with the love and support they need. Additionally, dedicating myself to my career has allowed me to channel my energy into something productive and fulfilling.

Life's unexpected challenges will always be present, but it is our mindset that determines how we navigate through them. These challenges are opportunities for growth and self-discovery.

By maintaining a positive outlook and a resilient spirit, I am confident that I can overcome any obstacle that comes my way.

And I am hopeful that the universe will align the right person and the right time for me. Until then, I will continue to focus on building a fulfilling life for myself and those around me. I am excited for what the future holds.

My healing journey:

I am determined to break the cycle of poverty that has plagued my family for generations.

With every step I take, I am driven by the love and responsibility I feel towards my children and my family back in Cameroon. They have endured so much pain and suffering, and it is my duty to create a brighter future for them. I want to show them that there is more to life than the hardships we have known.

I yearn to be a beacon of hope, a guiding light that illuminates a better tomorrow. I want to inspire my family to see beyond their current circumstances and believe in the possibilities that lie ahead. Through my personal growth and healing, I hope to show them that it is never too late to start anew.

As I pour my heart and soul into this mission, I find solace in my faith. I pray to God, seeking His blessings and guidance in every endeavor I undertake. I know that with His divine intervention, I can overcome any obstacle and bring about the change I so desperately seek.

My maternal relatives are at the forefront of my mind. I want to uplift them from the chains of poverty and offer them a life filled with opportunities and abundance. I want to be the catalyst for their transformation, the one who shows them that dreams can become a reality.

In this pursuit, I am aware that the road ahead may be challenging. There will be setbacks and moments of doubt, but I am prepared to face them head-on. I am armed with determination, resilience, and an unwavering belief in the power of change.

I am committed to my personal growth and healing, not only for myself but for the generations that will follow. I want my children and my family to look back on this journey and see it as a turning point, a moment when we broke free from what held us captive for far too long.

I am ready to embrace the challenges, to learn from my past, and to create a future that is filled with hope, abundance, and love.

Going to therapy:

I have also learned to set boundaries and communicate my needs effectively, which has improved my relationships with others. I no longer feel the need to constantly please everyone and put their needs before my own. Instead, I prioritize my own well-being and understand that taking care of myself is not selfish, but necessary for my own happiness and mental health.

Through therapy, I have gained a better understanding of my past traumas and how they have shaped me. I have learned to forgive myself for the mistakes I made and the pain I endured. This forgiveness has allowed me to let go of the anger and resentment that had been weighing me down for so long.

In addition to therapy, I have also found solace in various self-care practices. Whether it's practicing mindfulness and meditation, engaging in creative outlets like painting or writing, or simply taking long walks in nature, these activities have become essential in my healing. They provide me with a sense of peace and allow me to reconnect with myself on a deeper level.

As I continue to grow and heal, I am confident in my ability to face any challenges that come my way and to continue to prioritize my own well-being.

Therapy has truly been a transformative experience for me. It has given me the tools and support I needed. I am grateful for the guidance and understanding of my therapist, as well as the unwavering support of my loved ones. With their help, I have become the best version of myself, and I am excited to continue this journey of self-discovery and growth.

Why Georgia?

My mother had spent her entire life in the United States, residing in Washington DC as an adult. When it came time for me to join her, she reached out to a friend in DC to provide me with a place to stay. Unfortunately, her friend was unable to accommodate me, leaving me in a difficult situation with nowhere to go. I needed a place to land in order to complete my residency paperwork, so I had to rely on my own connections. Luckily, I knew people in Cameroon, and through a friend whose father had many connections, a few calls were made on my behalf. I was simply searching for a temporary place to stay.

One person I reached out to explained that it fell through due to personal circumstances. However, fate seemed to intervene when I boarded a plane to DC and discovered that someone on the same flight was headed to Atlanta. We struck up a conversation, and I mustered the courage to ask if her mother could assist me. Generously, her mother agreed to take me to their home. I sat there for two hours, grateful for their kindness. Eventually, my mother called her friend, who agreed to drop me off at the train station.

At this point, I was still unfamiliar with the English language, struggling to communicate with broken English. A man named Guy came to pick me up from the train station and provided me with specific instructions. He advised me to only speak to the police and cautioned against seeking assistance from anyone else. He emphasized the importance of staying alert and keeping my mind engaged. I was around twenty-one years old.

After finally arriving in Atlanta, Georgia, I decided to settle there and pursue my education. It was in Atlanta that I met my ex-husband. Although our marriage eventually ended in divorce, I remained determined to continue my education while working full-time and being a devoted mother to our two beautiful children.

Moving to Massachusetts and then New Hampshire:

In 2010, I made the decision to leave behind my life and marriage in Georgia and start fresh in Massachusetts. The transition was far from easy. Initially, I stayed at a friend's house in Massachusetts while waiting for my car and belongings to arrive from Georgia. It also served as a temporary base for me to start my new job and search for a place to live. During this time, I resided in Worcester and commuted to work in Malden.

Living in someone else's home, especially with children, proved to be quite an experience. Despite my friend's warm welcome, I felt out of place and uncomfortable. I longed for my own space and eagerly awaited the opportunity to leave. Finally, after two weeks, my car arrived, and I could begin working while also searching for a reliable babysitter for my children. Since my friend had her own work commitments, it was challenging to rely on her to constantly care for my kids. After a difficult search, we managed to find someone trustworthy to look after my son. My older daughter attended school and could go home with my friend's children, eliminating the need for a sitter.

As I worked long hours, my girlfriend kindly picked up my son from the sitter. She expressed concerns about the environment and urged me to find an alternative. Around this time, my mother had relocated to Indianapolis, and with the end of the school year approaching, she suggested I bring the children to her and focus on finding a permanent place to stay. I had no money, having left my marital home without taking any funds. I had to wait for my first and second paychecks to secure an apartment. Eventually, I managed to find a place for my children and myself in Woburn, Massachusetts, which conveniently had a short fifteen-minute commute to my workplace. Once my belongings arrived, I was ready to retrieve my children, but my mother insisted I wait until a month before school started. I am forever grateful for her gesture, as it allowed me to establish myself.

Despite the distance, I had to travel back and forth between Massachusetts and Georgia to fight for custody of my children against my ex-husband. Thankfully, I was eventually granted custody, and this victory brought me a sense of relief and reassurance.

With custody of my children secured, I could finally focus on building a new life for us in Massachusetts. The first few months in our new apartment were filled with unpacking boxes, setting up bedrooms, and making the space feel like home. It was a small, cozy place, but it was ours, and that made all the difference.

As the school year approached, I enrolled my children in a nearby school and started to get involved in the community. I joined parent-teacher associations, attended school events, and made an effort to meet other parents. It was important for me to create a support system for my children and myself. Being an active member of the community helped us feel more connected.

Work was demanding, but I was grateful for the stability it provided. It allowed me to provide for my children and give them the opportunities they deserved. It wasn't always easy juggling work and parenting, but I was determined to give my children the best life possible.

Over time, Massachusetts started to feel like home. We explored the beautiful landscapes, visited historical sites, and embraced the vibrant culture. The change of scenery was refreshing, and it opened our eyes to new experiences and possibilities. We made friends, created memories, and slowly but surely we built a life that was filled with love and happiness.

Massachusetts was the place where destiny brought me together with the father of my third child. Our relationship was a beautiful blend of love and respect, but unfortunately, our egos overshadowed our ability to fully support each other romantically. Despite this, we decided to remain close friends and raise our youngest daughter together, demonstrating to her that although we couldn't be a couple, our bond was rooted in love and respect. This was the first relationship where I felt liberated to express myself without fear of being dismissed, as I could openly share my thoughts and feelings, knowing that he would listen and collaborate with me to find solutions. Even today, the father of my youngest daughter and I maintain an exceptional friendship and co-parenting dynamic.

We have always prioritized our daughter's well-being and

happiness above all else. Despite not being together romantically, we have managed to maintain a strong bond as friends and co-parents.

Our decision to raise our daughter together, despite not being in a romantic relationship, was not an easy one. However, we both understood that our love and respect for each other could still create a nurturing environment for our child. We want her to grow up knowing that even though her parents are not together, they still love and support each other.

We communicate openly and honestly, always striving to find common ground and make decisions together.

Our daughter is witnessing the love and respect we have for each other. She sees that love can exist in different forms and that co-parenting can be a successful and fulfilling arrangement.

As our daughter continues to grow, we remain committed to providing her with a stable and loving environment. We attend school events and extracurricular activities together, always showing a united front.

Our friendship has also been a source of support and comfort for both of us. We have been there for each other through life's ups and downs, offering a listening ear and a shoulder to lean on. We have built a strong foundation of trust and understanding, which has allowed us to navigate the challenges of co-parenting with grace and compassion.

While our romantic relationship may not have worked out, we are grateful for the deep love and respect we share as friends and co-parents. Our daughter is a constant reminder of the beautiful connection we once had and the enduring bond we continue to nurture. Together, we have created a loving and supportive family dynamic that will always be there for our daughter, no matter what.

Looking back, leaving behind my old life in Georgia was a difficult decision, but it was also the best decision I ever made. It allowed me to break free from a toxic marriage and create a fresh start. Massachusetts became our sanctuary, a place where we could heal, grow, and thrive.

Massachusetts will always hold a special place in our hearts, as it was the place where I found myself and discovered the strength within me to overcome any obstacle that comes my way.

In 2014, I made the decision to relocate to Nashua, New Hampshire. Nashua is a vibrant and welcoming city that has provided me with countless opportunities and a sense of belonging. From the moment I arrived, I knew that this was a place where we could truly build a life.

One of the things that immediately drew me to Nashua was its strong sense of community. The people here are friendly, supportive, and always willing to lend a helping hand. Whether it's through local events, volunteer opportunities, or simply striking up a conversation with a neighbor, I have found that the people of Nashua genuinely care about one another and are invested in making this city a better place for everyone.

Another aspect of Nashua that I love is its natural beauty. The city is nestled in the picturesque Merrimack Valley, surrounded by rolling hills, lush forests, and scenic rivers. There are numerous parks and outdoor spaces where I can go to relax, unwind, and enjoy the beauty of nature. Whether it's taking a leisurely stroll along the Nashua Riverwalk or exploring the trails at Mine Falls Park, there is always a new adventure waiting just outside my doorstep.

Nashua is also a city that values education and provides excellent opportunities for personal and professional growth. The school system here is top-notch, with dedicated teachers and a wide range of extracurricular activities for students to participate in. As a parent, I am grateful for the quality education that my children receive and the support they have received from their teachers and peers.

In addition to its strong educational system, Nashua is also home to a thriving business community. There are numerous job opportunities in a variety of industries, and the city is known for its entrepreneurial spirit. I have been able to start my own business here, but because of that business being unique, I have not receive much support from the community of Nashua as I have hoped. The locals here have their own palate, and they tend not to venture to trying food from Africa.

One of the things that sets Nashua apart from other cities is its rich cultural scene. There are numerous art galleries, theaters, and music venues where I can immerse myself in the arts. The city also hosts a variety of festivals and events throughout the year, celebrating everything from music and food to culture and history. These events not only provide entertainment but also bring the community together and foster a sense of unity and pride. While I appreciate the recent efforts made by the city to host multicultural events, I believe there is still room for improvement. It would be wonderful if they could provide more opportunities for cultural inclusion and diversity, similar to the recent event they organized for the first time. By doing so, they would not only demonstrate their commitment to embracing different cultures but also address the current lack of support for the African community.

Another aspect of Nashua that I like is its proximity to other major cities. Located just a short drive from Boston, Massachusetts, and Manchester, New Hampshire, Nashua offers the best of both worlds. I can easily access the amenities and attractions of these larger cities while still enjoying the charm and tranquility of Nashua.

Overall, my move to Nashua has been a transformative experience. This city has provided me with a sense of belonging, a supportive community, and countless opportunities for personal growth. I am grateful for the friendships I have made, the experiences I have had, and the memories I have created here. Nashua truly feels like home, and I am excited to continue building a life here filled with love, happiness, and fulfillment. In time, I believe the city will strive to include the African community as part of its community.

Holding to the dream:

With faith in God, I believe that all things are possible.

Reaching for the stars, I remind myself of the dreams I had when I first started this business. I remember the passion that fueled me, the determination that pushed me forward, and the belief that I could create something extraordinary. It's true that the road has been tough, and there have been moments when I questioned my choices and doubted my abilities. But in those moments of doubt, I think about my children and the future I want to provide for them.

I want them to grow up knowing that anything is possible, that hard work and perseverance can lead to success. I want them to see their mother as a role model, someone who faced adversity head-on and never gave up. I want them to inherit not just financial stability, but also the values of resilience and determination.

So, I push through the sleepless nights and the constant stress. I remind myself that building a business is not just about making money, but about creating something that will outlast me. It's about leaving a mark on this world, no matter how small. It's about proving to myself and others that I am capable of achieving greatness.

Yes, there are times when I feel overwhelmed and exhausted. But I've learned to find strength in those moments of weakness. I reach out to my support system, whether it's friends, family, or fellow entrepreneurs who understand the struggles I face. Their encouragement and advice remind me that I'm not alone in this journey.

And so, I continue to bootstrap my business, finding creative ways to make it thrive despite limited resources. I seek out opportunities for growth and expansion, always keeping an eye on the horizon. I know that success doesn't come overnight, but I'm willing to put in the work and make the sacrifices necessary to achieve my goals.

Because at the end of the day, it's not just about the money or the accolades. It's about the legacy I'm building, the impact I'm making, and the example I'm setting for my children. It's about showing them that with determination, resilience, and a little bit of faith, they too can reach for the stars and create a life of which they're proud.

So, I wipe away the tears, put on a brave face, and continue. One day, I will look back and be grateful for every single drop of sweat shed along the way.

It's also about the impact I am making in people's lives. Through Mola Foods and Jals cuisine Bantu, I am not only providing delicious meals but also preserving and sharing the rich cultural heritage of my ancestors.

I am proud to be able to introduce people to the flavors and traditions of Bantu cuisine, to educate them about the history and significance behind each dish. It's a way of keeping our traditions alive and passing them down to future generations.

Knowing that I am contributing to the preservation of my culture fills me with a sense of purpose and fulfillment.

My faith in God has carried me through. I have learned to trust in His plan and to lean on Him for strength and guidance. He has shown me that I am capable of so much more than I ever imagined, and He has surrounded me with a community of supporters who believe in my vision.

I am grateful for every customer who walks through the doors of my restaurants, for every person who orders from my online store. Their patronage not only sustains my business but also fuels my passion to keep pushing forward. Their feedback and encouragement inspire me to constantly improve and innovate.

I am committed to staying true to my roots and to the values that have guided me. As I look ahead to the future, I know that the road ahead will not be easy, but I am prepared to face any challenges that come my way.

So, I thank God for His unwavering presence in my life, for the strength He has given me to overcome obstacles, and for the opportunities He has provided. And I thank each and every person who has supported my business, for believing in me and being a part of this incredible journey.

Together, we are creating something extraordinary. Together, we are building a legacy that will stand the test of time. And with God by my side and the support of my community, I know that the future holds endless possibilities.

I recently fell ill and was down for a week. During those seven days of illness, when I felt as though my world was crumbling, I realized that the business I had poured my heart and soul into did not hold the same significance as I had once believed. It became clear that my absence did not affect the world in the way I had imagined. No one was there to cover for me, and it was in that moment that I understood the importance of self-care and the need to prioritize my own well-being.

Your unwavering support and encouragement have meant the world to me. With a mix of emotions, I regretfully inform you that I will be temporarily closing our business in Nashua and taking a sabbatical. However, this closure does not mark the end of our journey. Instead, it presents an opportunity for me to step back, reflect, and re-evaluate our business strategy. This break will allow me to gain fresh perspectives and make necessary adjustments to ensure future success. Although it is a difficult decision, I am hopeful that this sabbatical will ultimately lead to a stronger and more resilient business when we return.

I have poured my heart and soul into this venture, hoping to make a difference and meet the needs of our community. Despite the incredible support from some of you, it has become clear that challenges of recruiting and finding dedicated individuals to join the service industry have taken a toll on me.

Continuing without human resources would only lead to burnout and exhaustion. It is not fair to myself or to the business to keep pushing forward without the mental and emotional capacity to do so.

I want to express my deepest gratitude to each and every one of you who believe in my vision and supports my business. Your loyalty and patronage is invaluable.

As I take this time for myself, I will reflect on my journey and explore new possibilities for the future. I am excited to discover what lies ahead and find a path that aligns with my passions and aspirations. Your continued support and understanding during this transition mean the world to me.

While I embark on this sabbatical, I want to emphasize that it is not the end of my business journey. Instead, it is a period of rejuvenation and growth. I am filled with hope and optimism for what lies ahead. During this time, I will take the opportunity to recharge and refocus, ensuring that I come back stronger than ever. I look forward to assembling a dedicated team and approaching the relaunch with a renewed mindset, armed with valuable lessons learned and a clear vision for the future. This sabbatical is merely a stepping stone towards a brighter and more successful chapter in my business.

Knowing that I am my own legacy has brought a sense of peace and contentment. The knowledge that my children will forever carry the lessons and values I have taught them fills me with immense pride. It is not the wealth or success of my business that will define me, but rather the love, compassion, and wisdom I have imparted upon my children.

As I reflect on the years that have passed, I recognize the sacrifices I have made. The countless hours spent building my business have left little time for rest and relaxation. Vacations have become a distant memory, overshadowed by the constant drive to achieve more. It is time to shift my focus and step back from the business I have created and allow time for redirection. It's time for the universe to do its thing. While our current location may not have been ideal for my business, this experience has taught me a valuable lesson about the significance of due diligence when selecting a location. It is crucial to thoroughly observe and assess a potential place, considering factors such as foot traffic, the performance of neighboring businesses, and the overall suitability for business growth. I have come to realize that even the most effective marketing strategies can only take us so far if the positioning does not attract sufficient traffic. Moving forward, I will apply these lessons to ensure that our next location is carefully chosen, setting us up for success and driving more customers to our business.

This year in particular has tested my resilience and strength. Yet, through it all, I have found solace in the belief that God always has the last laugh. It is through these trials that I have grown, learned, and discovered the true meaning of success.

So, as I embark on this new chapter, I do so with a renewed sense of purpose. I will focus on nurturing myself and raising my last born, cherishing every moment and savoring the simple pleasures that life has to offer. And with God by my side, I know that the future holds even greater possibilities than I could have ever imagined. I am filled with anticipation to discover what lies ahead and how this break from the business will shape my entrepreneurial perspective. Stepping away provides an opportunity for introspection and growth, allowing me to reassess my strategies and make necessary changes to foster the future growth of the business. I am excited to see how this time away will inspire fresh ideas and innovative approaches that will propel the business to new heights. The journey ahead holds immense potential, and I am eager to embrace it with a renewed sense of purpose and determination.

My life as a single mother:

Despite the challenges and hardship I faced as a single mother, I am grateful for the blessings of my three children. Raising them alone without any outside help or strong family ties has been a daunting and sometimes frightening task. There were countless times when I had to bring my children to work with me because I couldn't afford a babysitter. They would sit quietly in the back of the classroom while I taught, or I would rely on the kindness of a colleague to watch over them while I worked to provide for our family.

I always felt a deep sense of responsibility as their mother to ensure they had a better life, even if it meant sacrificing my own needs. There were times when money was incredibly tight, and I would prioritize feeding my children after paying all the bills. I would go without so that they could have enough to eat. This was something I had experienced back in Cameroon, but I never imagined I would face it here in America.

The reality of the wages compared to the cost of living in the USA was a harsh wake-up call. It was disheartening to see how little I earned in relation to the expenses required to provide a decent life for my children. I remained determined to give them the best opportunities possible.

I sought out resources and support wherever I could find them. Through it all, I held onto the belief that my hard work and perseverance would eventually lead to a brighter future for my children.

The struggles:

Looking back, I realize that the struggles I faced as a single mother have shaped me into the strong and resilient woman I am today. They have taught me the true meaning of sacrifice and the power of a mother's love. And while the journey has been far from easy, I am proud of the legacy I am building for my children.

I want them to know that no matter the obstacles they face in life, they have the strength within them to overcome. I want them to understand the value of hard work and perseverance, and to never take anything for granted. Most importantly, I want them to know that they are loved unconditionally and that their mother will always be there for them, no matter what.

So, despite the low wages and the challenges of raising children alone in a foreign country, I continue to push forward. I continue to work hard and provide for my family, knowing that the sacrifices I make today will pave the way for a brighter future. With the love and support of my children, I am confident that we will overcome any obstacle that comes our way.

Breaking out of my shell:

I've come to understand that being both introverted and extroverted has its advantages in different situations. When I'm at home, I find solace in my own company, enjoying the quiet and introspective moments that recharge my energy. It's during these times that I can fully immerse myself in my thoughts, hobbies, and personal interests.

When I step out into the public sphere, whether it's for work or social gatherings, I've learned to tap into my extroverted side. As a business person, I've realized the importance of networking, building connections, and being approachable. This requires me to step out of my comfort zone and engage in conversations with people around me.

At first, it was a challenge for me to find the right words or initiate conversations, but with practice, I've become more comfortable in social settings. I've learned to observe and listen attentively, finding common ground or interesting topics to discuss. This switch from introversion to extroversion has allowed me to connect with others, build relationships, and expand my professional network.

While it may seem contradictory to be both introverted and

extroverted, I've come to appreciate the balance it brings to my life. The introverted side allows me to reflect, recharge, and delve into my own thoughts, while the extroverted side enables me to connect with others, share ideas, and collaborate.

In the business world, being able to adapt and switch between these two traits has proven to be an asset. It allows me to understand different perspectives, empathize with others, and effectively communicate my ideas. By embracing both sides of my personality, I've found a unique approach to navigating the complexities of the professional world.

Ultimately, being introverted and extroverted has taught me the importance of self-awareness and adaptability. It's about recognizing the needs of the situation and adjusting my behavior accordingly. Whether it's finding solace in my own thoughts or engaging in meaningful conversations, I've learned to embrace the duality within me and use it to my advantage in both personal and professional endeavors.

Friendships:

It's important for me to have friends who understand the concept of reciprocity in friendship. I believe that if I make an effort to listen and be there for my friends, I should expect the same level of support from them. Unfortunately, I have experienced one-sided friendships in the past, where I was always the one reaching out and offering support, but when I needed them, they were nowhere to be found. This imbalance taught me the importance of detaching myself and learning to be independent.

Some may view my preference for solitude as loneliness, but I see it as finding peace within myself. True friendship cannot be forced; it is a precious gift that should be cherished. If I am fortunate enough to have a loyal friend who stands by me through thick and thin, I consider it a valuable bond that must be nurtured.

In a friend, I highly value confidentiality. When we share our thoughts and experiences, I expect them to remain between us. I don't appreciate it when friends share our private conversations with others, as if it were casual gossip. If I wanted everyone to know, I would simply post it on social media. So, when I confide in someone, I hope they understand the importance of keeping our conversation private.

It has come to my attention that some people use the information I share with them as topics of conversation with their partners, husbands, or boyfriends. This raises a question in my mind: am I a friend of their partner or theirs? Why would they share my personal business without my consent? To me, this behavior demonstrates a lack of loyalty and creates cracks in the foundation of our friendship. It makes me question whether I can trust them with my feelings, or anything related to my life.

In conclusion, I believe that true friendship is built on mutual support, trust, and respect. It is a bond that should be treasured and nurtured. I value friends who understand the importance of confidentiality and who respect the boundaries of our conversations. Ultimately, I seek friendships that bring me peace of mind and make me feel valued and understood.

My spiritual life:

Throughout my journey on this earth, I have experienced fluctuations in my spirituality. There have been times when I wholeheartedly believed in God, and other times when I turned to worldly things, searching for fulfillment. Finding a balance between the two has been a constant challenge for me over the years.

To navigate this world and all its ungodly influences, I need to prioritize my spirituality. I need to surround myself with God's protection and love. Accepting that Christ died on the cross for my sins and that I am redeemed has been a pivotal moment in my spiritual journey. It has allowed me to reconnect with my faith on a deeper level.

Now, I approach decision-making differently. I no longer make choices without first bringing them to God for discernment. In the past, I made decisions without seeking His guidance, and they often ended up causing me pain or leading me down the wrong path. But now, I have learned that when I pray and ask God for guidance, solutions and opportunities present themselves that lead me towards a successful and fulfilling path.

Prayer has become an integral part of my life. I rely on it more than ever to guide me and alleviate stress. It keeps me grounded and reminds me of the bigger picture. Through prayer, I find solace and strength to face the challenges that come my way.

In this world filled with distractions and temptations, my spirituality is not something to be neglected or put on the back burner. It is a vital aspect of my life that brings me peace, purpose, and a sense of belonging. By prioritizing my relationship with God, I travel earthly journey with a renewed sense of purpose and a deep connection to something greater than myself.

The power of forgiveness:

Do I take matters into my own hands? That was a question that constantly lingered in my mind as I navigated through life's challenges. Growing up with a hardened exterior, I believed that seeking revenge was the only way to protect myself from being hurt again. But as I matured, I began to question the validity of this mindset.

Holding onto grudges and seeking retribution only weighed me down, trapping me in a cycle of negativity. It was as if I was carrying a heavy burden on my shoulders, preventing me from experiencing true peace and happiness. That's when I discovered the power of forgiveness.

Forgiveness was not about condoning the actions of those who wronged me. It was about freeing myself from the chains of anger and resentment. It was about choosing to let go and move forward, not for their sake, but for my own well-being.

I understood that by forgiving, I was not excusing their behavior or allowing them to escape consequences. Instead, I was releasing myself from the grip of bitterness and allowing myself to heal. It was a way of reclaiming my own power and refusing to let their actions define me.

As I embraced forgiveness, I also began to trust in the concept of karma. The universe has its own way of balancing things out. Those who inflict pain and harm onto others will eventually face the consequences of their actions, whether it be through divine intervention or the natural course of life.

So, instead of seeking revenge, I chose to let go and let karma take its course. I found solace in knowing that justice would prevail, even if it didn't happen on my timeline or in the way I expected. I surrendered the need to control the outcome and placed my faith in a higher power.

Now, when someone does me wrong, I no longer feel the need to retaliate. I trust that the universe will handle it in due time. This newfound perspective has brought me a sense of inner peace and allowed me to focus on nurturing my own soul.

In the end, forgiveness has become my greatest strength. It has transformed me from a person consumed by anger and vengeance into someone who radiates compassion and understanding. I have learned that true power lies not in seeking revenge, but in choosing forgiveness and embracing the freedom it brings.

A look ahead:

Living solely for the expectations of others has left me feeling empty and unfulfilled. It's as if I have been living in the shadows, suppressing my own desires and dreams in order to please those around me. But now, standing at this crucial junction of my life, I am determined to break free from this cycle and prioritize my own happiness.

It's time to embark on a journey of self-discovery, to explore the depths of my own passions and interests. I want to uncover the things that truly ignite a fire within me, the activities that bring me joy and fulfillment. Whether it's pursuing a long-lost hobby, delving into a new career path, or simply taking the time to indulge in activities that bring me peace, I am ready to embrace what makes me happy.

This newfound pursuit of happiness is not meant to be selfish or isolated. As I begin to prioritize my own well-being, I understand the importance of sharing that light with others around me. After all, true happiness is often found in the connections we forge and the impact we have on those we encounter.

I want to inspire others to also seek their own happiness, to break free from societal expectations and live authentically. By leading by example, I hope to encourage my loved ones and those around me to explore their own passions, to listen to their hearts, and to prioritize their own happiness.

This journey will not be without its challenges. There may be moments of doubt and uncertainty, as I navigate uncharted territories and step outside of my comfort zone. I am determined to persevere, to push through the fear and embrace the unknown, because I know that true happiness lies on the other side.

No longer will I let the expectations of others dictate my every move. It's time to prioritize my own happiness, to shine brightly and illuminate the world around me. In doing so, I hope to inspire others to do the same, creating a community of individuals who are unapologetically living their best lives.

I hope that this memoir will provide me with a sense of inspiration and motivation. I hope it will remind me of the strength and resilience I possess and encourage me to keep pushing forward despite any obstacles that may come my way. I hope it will serve as a reminder that life is full of ups and downs, but it is how we navigate through them that truly matters.

Moving forward in my life, I hope to continue growing and evolving as an individual. I hope to learn from my past experiences and use them as steppingstones towards a brighter future. I hope to cultivate meaningful relationships and surround myself with people who uplift and support me. I hope to find true love, someone who will stand by my side through thick and thin, and together, build a lasting and fulfilling relationship.

In terms of my business, I hope to see it flourish and become a success. If not, I hope it will always be an iconic moment in time in our society.

As a parent, my hope is for my children to find their own paths in life. I hope they discover their passions and pursue careers that bring them joy and fulfillment. I hope they form deep and meaningful connections with others and experience the beauty of love and companionship. I hope to be a guiding light for them, offering support and guidance whenever they need it.

Furthermore, I hope to use my experiences as a single mother to help others who may be facing similar challenges. I hope to create a support system for single mothers, providing them with resources and assistance to alleviate their burdens. I hope to empower them and show them that they are not alone in their journey.

Ultimately, my hope extends beyond my personal life. I hope for a better world, one where love triumphs over hate, and where humanity is valued above political agendas. I hope for a world where our children and grandchildren can thrive, free from the constraints of discrimination and inequality. I hope to contribute to this vision in any way I can, whether it be through advocacy, philanthropy, or simply spreading kindness and compassion.

So, while expectations may be strong, I choose to approach life with hope. Hope for better days, better opportunities, and a better world.

"For with God, nothing will be impossible"
- Luke 1:32

This is my grandmother Sophie

My Mother Rebecca

Milton Keynes UK
Ingram Content Group UK Ltd.
UKHW020616251123
433184UK00009B/129